Jubilant!

Contemplative Coloring for All People.

An exploration of original, hand drawn art by Angel Cheney.

Art is a beautiful medium for relaxation, stress relief, therapy, and enjoyment. It is our hope that as you travel through these pages you will be encouraged by what you find and experience. Some of the pages include areas of white space where you can add your own thoughts, dreams, or doodles. Enjoy!

While working on each page try adding the words "I AM" to the theme word for the page and repeating the phrase while you color. For example, "I am jubilant!"

About the artist:

Angel Cheney is an artist, singer/songwriter, poet, and author from the Indianapolis, IN area. She is passionate about taking people on a journey with her through art, words, and music. Check out more of her work at:

www.angelcheney.com

© 2016 Hummingbird Media

Stay tuned!
Exciting new books of
Contemplative Coloring
for All People
COMING SOON!

light hearted

MAGNIFICENT

LOVED

BEAUTIFUL

Vivacious

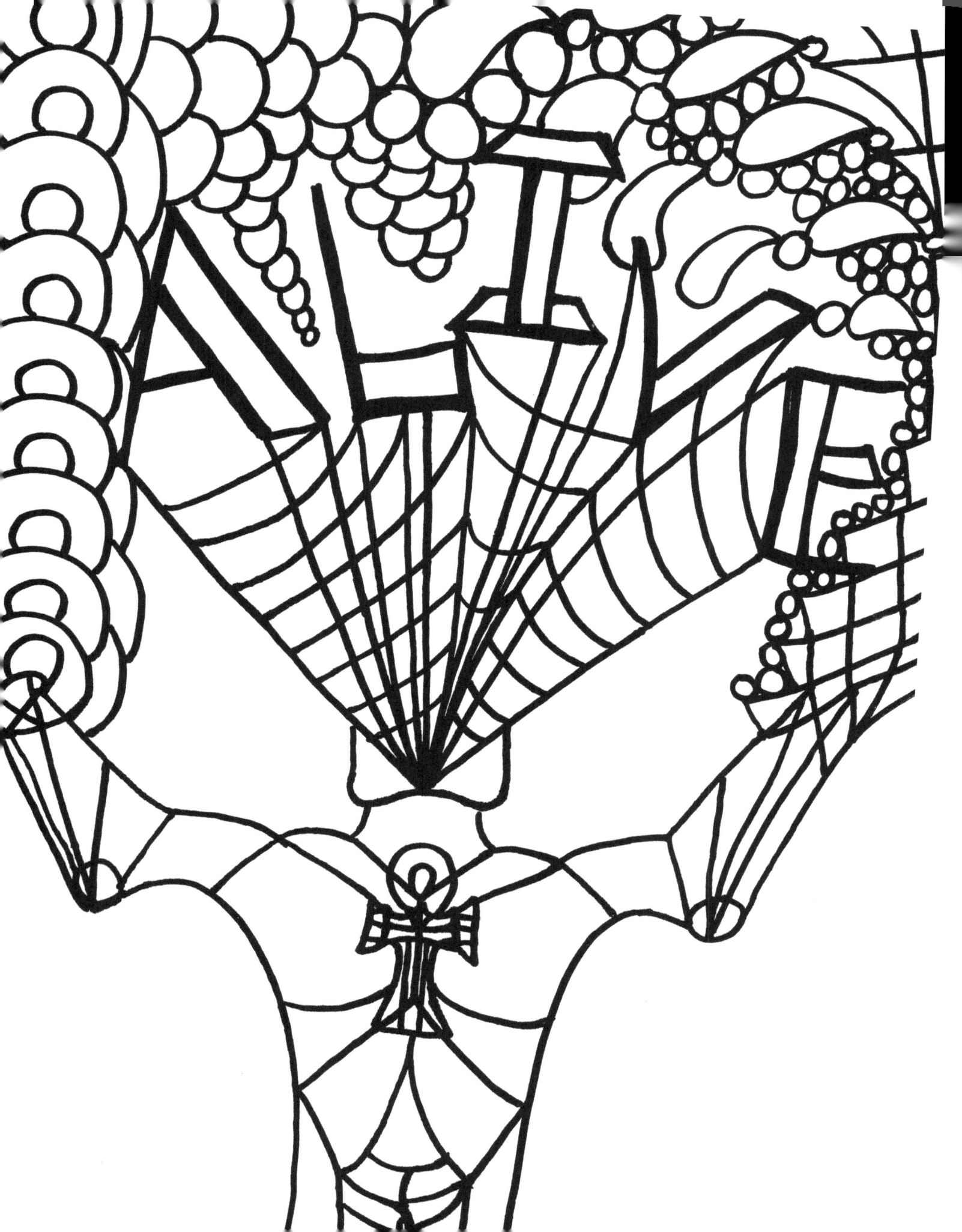

DYNAMIC

FREE

Exquisite

ENOUGH

VIBRANT

RENEWED

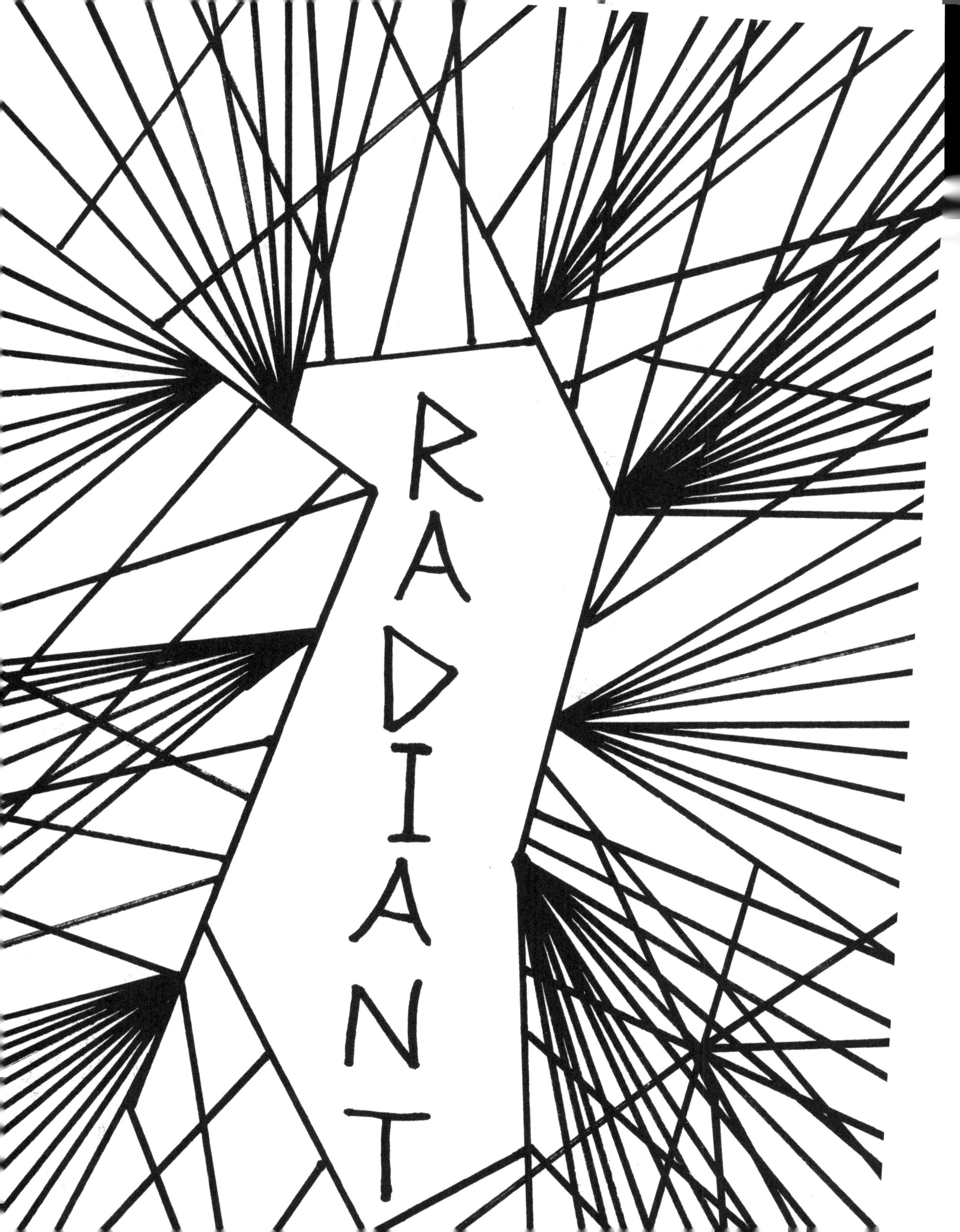
RADIANT

INSPIRATION

Passionate